Barcode Kingpin : The emerging science of algorithmic hedge fund trading

As seen @ www.facedollar.co.uk

ATS = Automated Trading System

The path of most resistance : Winning the Big Game

"There is a spider and it is alive and it LIVES. And it controls all commerce on earth. This tiny little parasite." m3e

I first became interested in the markets as a way of gaining financial independence around the year 2000 while living in London and working as a sales consultant for a small photography firm selling portraiture in the West End. Alone in the world and finding that my pay packet barely stretched to cover the basic necessities of life, let alone having any fun, and without any real sense of how I was going to accomplish it, I began in earnest to start piecing together the parts of a strategy I had to get out of the sales racket and into what I felt must surely be a more lucrative game : the world markets. At the time I had little inkling of what a long and drawn out path it would be but my naivety coupled with boundless enthusiasm was a potent mix.

I fancy that if I'd gone to an MIT type technical school then I would have almost certainly made automation in the marketplace my dissertation thesis piece. I got my first computer when I was about eight years old and ever since then I've been fascinated by the things. My father is actually listed on my birth certificate in 1976 as a computer scheduler which in those days must have been a pretty rare occupation to be in. So it's absolutely fair to say that programming computers is in my blood and being a chip off the old block I was determined to follow in my father's footsteps and become a systems analyst.

Ever since I saw Kramer write a coffee table book on Seinfeld, (the book that actually turns into a coffee table), I've had the desire to publish a book on trading. I envisioned for my efforts a sort of cross between Steal This Book meets Salem's Lot. In contrast with the relentlessly grim and somewhat gloomy world of financial commentary, business could become an endlessly fascinating subject for learning if only there were a way to place it within the context of the bigger game we like to call life. A game that I became fascinated with at an early age and which ultimately led me to fortune. In this game analogies, puzzles and problem solving all contribute to a better understanding of trading and maths theory. As a guy I once knew once said to me "good trading, like good bullshit, is a science AND an art".

The end result of all my work is this book which ties together my interests in computer hacking, networks and programming, occult banking practices and conspiracy theory into a nice neat little package that I've always had the desire to write. My goal in writing it is simple. To make a book which is a one-stop shop for the aspiring trader to go from novice to relative mastery of the subject in the shortest time possible. I can confidently say that you will find information in this book that you will not find in any other book currently published and that very fact should tell you something about how coveted this kind of financial information really is.

From that first bite of forbidden fruit quite some years ago now when I first made the realisation that spontaneous wealth creation is like a kind of magic which can be mastered in the same way as mastering a musical instrument or a complex language. To this book, which I hope will encourage people to follow that same rabbit down that same rabbit hole and break out into a new world of opportunities they never previously had perceived existed. If even one person takes that leap of faith into the unknown then all my efforts will have surely been worth it.

Justin Fisher (aka : aNONYmouse) , Tel Aviv , 2015

1

Sticks and Stones may break my bones but names will never hurt me.

I had long considered the idea that I should write a book on how to build a trading system but it would be five long years of trial and error before I would perfect my system to the point where I felt I could comfortably lecture others on the finer points of this rather arcane sub branch of masonry. Indeed the very secretive nature of this profession made me constantly reassess the likely ramifications of publishing a book full of such traditionally taboo revelations. In the end though good old fashioned no nonsense greed intervened and made the choice an easy one. The revelation that trend Tracker version 1.0 (my working title at that time for the system I would ultimately describe herein) could make me the next Bill Gates made the choice an easy one. If only I could market it effectively and make the world understand how perfect a piece of software it really was my progression from small time trader to hedge fund supremo would be assured. I didn't just want to be the mouse that got the cheese. I would be the CAT that got the MICE that got the cheese. I honestly think that it should indeed be as popular a product as Windows is. The truth however, is that just like building your own light saber, interest in this kind of programming tends to be confined to a small elite of hobbyists and Boffins rather than being offered for sale in the mass market like so many McDonalds cheeseburgers.

Part of the problem I believe is THE system. The one that nobody ever mentions is the proverbial elephant in the room is so hopelessly arcane and obtuse that most well informed traders are absolutely not open to discussing their methods in anything but vague and guarded terms. Since the business of money is typically a secretive and covert business which is innately and powerfully tied into a hidden and all encompassing heirarchy that really gets to the very source of all corruption itself. For this reason the old law of omerta is frequently cited as a main reason why very little light seems to ever get shed on the hidden machinations of these let's face it GIGANTIC GODDAM MATHS BASED SYSTEMS. Like joining the mob it sometimes seems that once you're in, your in for life and can never get out.

It's funny but although you can pick up a book and hear Stephen Hawking expound his latest theories on the nature of chaos and the origins of the universe, it seems that you can't for love nor money find a decent book on algorithms and how to program your life in order to be successful. Being somewhat charitable by nature and with the old adage about teaching a man to fish to feed him for a lifetime foremost in my thoughts I am compelled to fill this void in the hope that I can in some small way make a worthwhile contribution to the field of investment science. If Bill Gates can pledge billions of dollars to help the poor then perhaps I too can make a worthwhile contribution to society with my knowledge in the absence of any actual funds to contribute. Or something like that anyway.

So as mentioned NOBODY wants to talk about the science behind the math and the math behind the science for "reasons so obtuse as to border on occult" to quote my favourite science fiction author William Gibson. But what if that very fact meant that the rewards for someone who was suitably prepared to "spill the beans" and "let the cat out of the bag" were enough to bring them out of the safety of their anonymous existences and put pen to paper. "Would anybody REALLY care?" I wondered out loud to nobody in particular.

This little piggy went to market.

The revelation that the solution isn't necessarily in the box but rather in the band meant that it dawned on me quite quickly that it would be potentially more lucrative to sell my system via a book and website rather than just simply trading it myself. So I began reading books on trading and researching diligently while still holding down full-time employment and plotting my path to success and fortune. Although the industry of desktop trading was still in its early formative stages in those days, it was experiencing a kind of Wild West gestation period as a huge tidal wave of change swept through the world of computing. A kind of perfect storm had developed preceding a new world order of golden age thinking and technology. To be a player all you needed to know was the rules of engagement.

As the 20th century drew to a close a combination of the birth of mainstream broadband Internet access together with the rapid growth of online industry and cheaper more powerful desktop computing had combined to create a once-in-a-lifetime boom of biblical proportions. The NASDAQ index composite of US technology stocks began a rapid inexorable rise. The index which in 1997 had been capitalised at less than 1000 hit a peak of 5130 March 2000. Companies like WorldCom and Oracle the US database firm rode this wave of exuberant buying all the way as a new wave of Internet entrepreneur sought to capitalise on this brave new frontier of Internet commerce now increasingly becoming the mainstay of individuals as well as big business. Worldwide the rush was on to secure a site on the information superhighway and stake a claim to what was essentially a land rush for virtual real estate. Essentially what was occurring was that technology and especially broadband internet connectivity had finally become cheap and powerful enough to migrate from the offices of big business and government into the homes of ordinary people. Although trading had existed prior to this time it was plagued by technological limitations, poor quality software and high commissions. In this new electronic frontier anyone with the knowhow and a little capital could now compete on a level playing field with old established mainstays of the industry such as banks and hedge funds.

A long time mainstay of the large banks and investment firms such as Goldman Sachs and JP Morgan,Morgan Stanley et al, the placing at the behest of individuals with computers the means to transact automated business signalled a tidal change in exactly who was now participating in the big game. The democratisation of technology-based trading could not have been more obvious if you proclaimed it from the neon billboards of Times Square. Indeed that was exactly what was happening as a huge wave of previously dormant household capital flooded the markets chasing the next big thing in Internet commerce. A lot of dumb money came into the market at this time as a result of this seismic shift in exactly who was participating in the market. This movement of market capitalism into the hands of individuals as well as the traditional market participants marked a key turning point in the evolution of day trading for the masses and the market definitely stood up and took notice. Day trading as a watchword experienced its first tentative steps toward becoming a mature industry as new firms such as cyber trader and e trade began to cater for a new breed of sophisticated interactive trader sat at home in front of their desktops with live financial information flow at their fingertips.

Many hands make light work

Since the 1960s the holy grail of computing had been a simple one. If there's one thing computers are really good at above all others things it's process control. The endless repetition of simple, monotonous tasks. The gathering of large quantities of price information and processing it through cookie cutter programming was a process custom tailored to the new breed of powerful desktops coupled with broadband speed and large bandwidth. From a purely technology-based standpoint this was the revolution in home based trading the market had been waiting for. It had only recently become available in the home having previously required large IT budgets typically only found in government and big business who were the progenitors of this kind of Delta neutral arbitrage algorithmic trading via mainframe computing. Indeed the Internet itself had its beginnings amongst these same origins with the government backed Arpanet of the 1960s and 70s, being confined to large clumsy mainframe systems connected to each other with early telephony that was hardwired.

Thus the backbone infrastructure and technical know-how had been in place many years before the migration to mainstream desktop computing in the last years of the 20th century. The major difference between the early beginnings of the internet and now was that the profile of the average participant was so markedly different due to the internet moving into the household via broadband instead of the traditionally slow and cumbersome dial-up access. Think 15 minute waits to download a webpage and you can appreciate how painfully slow the early beginnings of the internet revolution in the early 90's really were.

The significance of this shift in participant demographics cannot be underestimated as it effectively unleashed a vast monopoly power and democratised it for around 7 billion people simultaneously in one mighty step. By connecting all these people and individual computers together and linking them to the various exchanges around the world a vast reservoir of constantly circulating hot money was instantly unleashed on the world stock exchanges, currency and commodity markets by individuals seeking to profit from the free exchange of price via the internet.

This was true democratic capitalism for the masses on an unprecedented, epic global scale. Because price is in a state of constant flux it has tremendous power to reshape and remould not just the financial landscape but the wealth distribution matrix of society itself. It is the true democratisation of the global wealth sharing model away from Big Business into the hands of the general public and represents a key turning point in the way that society as a whole earns income since it takes what was previously a monopoly power to exploit pricing inefficiencies and places it at the behest of anybody who knows how to exploit it using desktop computing and trading software. Panning for gold in the brave new frontier of twenty-first century capitalism. A tidal shift in the power sharing mechanism of the modern world.

Okkoms razor : The shortest distance between any 2 points is a straight line

Having witnessed the spectacular explosion in the fortunes of creators of such diverse names as Pets.com and Travelzoo during the initial upsurge of interest in this new phenomenon everyone was calling the worldwide web, it was perhaps inevitable that such stratospheric growth couldn't help but be vulnerable to a bursting of its bubble. So it was perhaps no great surprise when the tech wreck of 2001 caused a drastic drop in the fortunes of Silicon Valley. Overnight the fortunes of many investors crashed as quickly as they had risen and many of these squatters on the new information superhighway found their business models crushed under the awesome weight of economic reality. The fundamental factors behind the boom still remained however, and it was clear that financial systems trading as a concept was very much here to stay for the long haul.

It was behind this backdrop that I made my first tentative foray onto the Internet and into the realm of electronic free trading. I was certain that computers held the key to changing my life for the long haul if only I could harness their ability to do repetitive tasks on my behalf. If only you understand how to program them to do your job for you, I reasoned, the rewards would be immense. After all it's important to understand the power inherent in being able to get a computer to work a hundred and twenty hours per week on your behalf without any effort on your part. I mean when I was a kid having my own robot was considered the stuff of science fiction. These days though it was possible to build one that would vacuum the rug, serve you expensive cocktails and balance your check book, all before morning tea at 8. Or so my fantasy would have me believe. I simply had to have one!

The realities of being an automated Swing Trader though, is that teaching a robot computer to break-dance is deceptively easy and filled with potential pitfalls and obstacles which can take many *years* to overcome. Still the idea of being the next Wall Street quant savant and fulfilling my adolescent fantasy of being Mr city centre rock star trading guru refused to let go and so, in spite of the pitfalls, I pushed on insanely towards my goals. Shunning my friends and family and holing up in my bedroom to unlock the ancient secrets of monetary alchemy I pored over the minutiae of detail of this brave new world of financial science literally for *years* before I finally figured out the equation which would transform my life and make me rich and successful. That moment of epiphany resulted in this book which I intend to help those who can't spend four years at a University or college learning a bunch of largely useless facts in order to break into the industry that is hedge fund trading. Can't because time is money and life is too short to waste it.

Basically I hoped that by reading my book, accepting that speculation is as old as the hills, and that price action will always follow the same familiar pattern, you can free yourself from the bondage of modern life and unchain the ties that bind you. You will see then the truth of why money really does change everything and why there really is a massive ever growing gap in our society between the rich and the poor.

Fortunately right around the time that all this was happening (2000), the hedge fund industry was just starting to really throttle up. Guys were leaving their own firms to start funds and overnight internet start-ups began coming online in brute force. Companies like Napster were just beginning to really shake up the established order of industries such as music and entertainment . Suddenly kids who had spent their whole lives playing with computers were being taken seriously in a way they hadn't been previously. It was possible to put entire industries out of business with one deft keystroke as the power of computers to change the way people operated their businesses became increasingly relevant to the new way of doing things. Naturally this was a source of potential friction between the old established orders and the new blood making its way into the workforce full of desire for change and eager to stake a claim in this gold rush of new ideas and talent. Wall Street firms too began to recognise the threat that these guys could pose to their old monopoly power structures as smaller firms such as E-trade and Cybertrader came into their own offering market access to the masses and bypassing the big expensive firms such as Goldman and UBS who had long been the gatekeepers guarding the doors to market connectivity.

Deus ex machina : translation, God from the machine

I had initially planned this book to be a straight out sober analysis of currency trading and systems design free from any references to societal and cultural influences. However this business is so intertwined within societal context that it naturally encompasses the obtuse and esoteric and any analysis of the system will tend to benefit from the tendency to reference the society in which it takes place. It's a tough call to make but in the end I chose to improvise some references to the biblical and occult context of the currency system at the risk of being derided as a crackpot because to me the two go hand in hand like sugar and spice. I guess I did this to highlight the importance of the system within its societal context rather than as just a simple nuts and bolts monetary system which tends to overwhelm people with its complexities rather than being approached as a lesson in simplicity winning out over elaborate solutions.

The fact that you're reading this book means that you are interested in learning how to trade like a hedge fund or that you're at the least curious about how the international monetary system works. On the other hand perhaps you just have an abiding interest in conspiracies and intrigue. At any rate the mechanics of how to be a market trader/player and what makes the money system work will be our topic for discussion. After all money makes the world go round so a good working knowledge of precisely how it moves is vital for any aspiring capitalist to get to grips with if he is to have any hope of getting rich. A guy I knew once told me "Money is round and it rolls. And it doesn't much care who it rolls too". I hope that as we progress the truth of this statement will become crystal clear to you.

So where does all this leave us or as they say where is the chase and how do I cut to it? Well at the risk of sounding like one of those shitty infomercials where all they do is promise you the world over and over again without actually ever TELLING YOU anything useful (great preparation for the day to day realities of life by the way) I'm going to begin with a little history lesson first.

In 1978 President Nixon removed the gold standard requiring the backing of new issues of currency with equivalent percentage backing in gold bullion. This new system of free-floating exchange and essentially unsecured credit creation gave birth to the system of International settlement of relative currency pricing known as the forex market. The significance of this change is this there is an estimated US$100 trillion in circulation in the world in paper form. Previously in order to print more money to issue into the general circulation would require a portion of the money to be backed by gold reserves but as modern computing emerged in the form of mainframes it became clear that the old system of gold standard backing was no longer acceptable.

There are many reasons why this is so but the main one that I want to get across is this. It (money) had, thanks to the invention of the computer and the birth of the network that would become the modern internet, henceforth ceased to exist in purely paper form but had instead become *a free-floating electronic entity.* Whilst a system of foreign exchange had existed for hundreds of years prior to that it was clear that in the brave new world of the network with its *free* floating point operations and positively charged electrons, Kansas would henceforth definitely be going bye bye.

The proliferation of the network and the spreading of computers into the home meant that in the new paradigm that was the coming digital world money creation would be moving from the realms of the physical such as gold to a new model where spontaneous wealth creation would become a theoretical rather than literal process. We can see this phenomenon at work even today with ever more exotic financial products and derivatives creating a system so vast and complex that it has long since moved beyond the ability of any one man or even one Government to understand it.

In this new model the value of a product (say Soybeans) was a free floating entity whose value could change by the second. Furthermore its value was assessed in terms of a currency (say USD) whose own value was itself changing by the millisecond .This creates an extremely complex system of interdependence and interrelationships between products and commodities whose value is in a constant state of flux due to ever shifting tides and geopolitical changes. And yet within this apparent maelstrom of chaos and anarchy that is the modern financial world, emerges a simple three line equation whose elegance and simplicity belies its awesome and all-consuming power. To bring order to chaos and control that which seems so totally chaotic. One ring to rule them all ...

The most valuable commodity I know of is information. So says Gordon Gecko but what is it specifically that makes information so powerful? Simply stated, in-formation is a specific way that information lines up where it suddenly makes complete and perfect sense. It's like one of those books they used to have called the magic eye where you stare and stare at these pictures for a long time and then all of a sudden when your eyes become relaxed in a certain specific way, from out of nowhere, out pops this goddam giant fucking sailing boat in 3d relief!

So now all the pieces of the puzzle were in place what was missing was a system of logic that would unscramble and make sense of the chaos that is raw price information flow. The Codex Hammer, cookie-cutter price distribution matrix itself. A system of algebraic explanation that would end once and for all the debate over exactly why does the early bird get the worm and exactly how does a stitch in time save nine. The original red herring crossed with smoking gun all rolled into one nifty package for the modern trader. The age old quest to build a better mousetrap and reinvent the wheel.

First though a quick history lesson on the market. It is often said that speculation is as old as the hills. As long as there have been markets for goods and services there have been speculators attempting to profit from price movement. Dutch tulips is one of the earliest forms of market during the 1600s Wall Street in the 1930's, the stock market crash of 1987. All throughout exhibited the same pricing model and all exhibited the same tendency towards moving in cycles from epic boom to spectacular bust, again and again. The key question though is why, and the answer is simple. Pricing is a universal construct which exhibits a familiar round robin structure which never changes. Jesse Livermore a well-known market player and ringer wrote a popular little book called "How to trade in stocks" which hints at these techniques by using what Livermore called pivot points. These are points at which fundamental change in market direction occurs. The key to being in business for the long term is that these pivot point demark the key shifts in trend from trending up to trending down. By using them as market timers we can profit over time from *price rotation* or the rotation of trends from up to down which occurs ceaselessly across all markets and all time frames as I've mentioned already. What matters to us as traders is which of these combinations of time frame and product have the best investment profile for us to profit from over time.

The simple truth though and what every market insider has known since the dawn of time is this. The market is rigged and exhibits the same loophole based pattern of price action again and again which never changes or alters, ever, period, never. And after reading this book you will hopefully understand this basic truth as well. That price is unceasing and unchanging in its patterning regardless of whether you are trading sugar, Treasury bonds, Microsoft or coffee beans, one-minute timeframes, daily timeframes, weekly timeframes, monthly timeframes. The one constant is change and this change can be expressed mathematically in an algebraic equation. The maths and sciences are more than mere abstract ideas in dusty old textbooks. They are fundamental instructions to *changing how your living your life and most importantly of all how you perceive the world around you.*

One constant in our civilisation is that of the fundamentally cyclical nature of all things. From phases of the moon, the movement of the tides, the orbit of the Earth around the sun, electrons around nucleus, the changing seasons, the one constant is THAT THE WORLD MOVES IN CYCLES OF REPETITION. Further these cycles can be micro cycles occurring thousands or even millions of times a second or macro cycles which can take thousands or even millions of years to complete a single revolution. Trends like this exist everywhere in nature. Circuitous and ceaselessly turning . Planets revolve in orbit and spin on an axis, the migrations of birds and animals. The overwhelming conclusion that I draw from observation of nature is that we live in a looped reality where everything moves in cycles.

 So extrapolating this notion to its inevitable conclusion as it relates to money we can say that if you want to make money in the markets over the long haul the most important shape to create to automate your future is a wheel. A circular ever turning cycle which functions like a feedback loop always moving in the same way again and again. So having established that cycles exist in nature it's perhaps not surprising then that similar cycles exist in the market. The business world of statistics and the market itself also move in trends and in cycles. These market cycles exist across all instruments and time frames in a completely consistent repetitive fashion as I have mentioned.

The real value of computers in relation to these cycles is to function as the cogs in the wheels of international business. Computing functions as a business tool linking together computers in a network in order to perform business between diverse competing parties. What is missing from the equation though is the thinking logic that creates the synergistic magic that is modern capitalism.

There is a great deal of conventional wisdom which says that pricing within a market is random and follows a directionless, nonsensical and illogical pattern of price behaviour which is impossible to predict with any degree of accuracy. This school of thought is known as random walk theory. Having correctly learned the ancient art of tape reading it will immediately become apparent that this idea is not even remotely accurate and completely at odds with those who can see clearly. For those attuned to the market and familiar with the art of tape reading it is patently nonsense. As Edwin LeFevre says in his thinly disguised biography of Jesse Livermore Reminiscences of a Stock Operator "It is nothing at all to be right on the market".

An Inquiry into the Nature and Causes of the Wealth of Nations, the seminal work by Adam Smith first published in 1776 made mention of a mysterious force at work within the free market system which Smith liked to call the "invisible hand". This work is considered by many students of economics the definitive turning point in the understanding of economic cycles and is also the underpinning of modern hedge fund trading methodology. It is essential as traders that we understand the invisible hand in purely logical terms via an algebraic equation since we are dealing in numbers and numbers are an absolute definitive science that should be able to be expressed in absolute definitive terms. This is what I understand to be tape reading although if you search on the internet you will likely find a different explanation for what tape reading is for reasons I shall elaborate on towards the end of this book. To my understanding tape reading and the invisible hand are one and the same thing.

There is a constantly repeating formula every trader should know and which should be as universally accepted as Einstein's equals MC squared theory of relativity and that is what I have nicknamed the Jinius formula. A simple three line mathematical equation which precisely explains Adam Smith's invisible hand in logical terms and articulates definitively the secret nature of price movement. Once you understand the implications of the fact that every free-floating price in the world can be hacked with this one distinct subroutine of sublime logic you can begin to understand the awesome primitive power that price plays in our daily lives and how powerful the Internet has become as a tool for the redistribution of wealth. Price really is priceless in the right hands.

So what it this revolutionary piece of logic which secretly controls our lives? This bargain akin to the free parking square on the monopoly board of life? Well it isn't the number 666 itself which is valuable, although it is a constant source of wonder to math magician types.   It is an abundant number. It is the sum of the first 36 numbers. Meaning that it is also the sum of all the numbers on a roulette wheel combined. It is also the sum of the first seven prime numbers squared. That number does however have a kind of spooky allure which intrigued me for the longest time until I figured out the reason why.

I envisaged the final product of my research as a kind of cable descrambler set-top black box. A "blackbox" is any kind of illicit electronic device which can bypass normal circuits: the original permitted its users to make long-distance phone calls without paying for them. This device would effectively be a Windows based pc with the specialist software loaded onto it. It would take any electronic cipher in this case a daily Euro/ US dollars and spit out over the long haul a number string that represents the results of said trading :+123 pips, −124pips +17 pips +212 pips, out to infinity. Out of this initial concept came the finished product which I am pleased to say is faithful to the desktop hedge fund in a box concept originally envisaged and capable of dismembering the market easily provided that my concept is followed to the tee.

The manipulation of money in this way is also a kind of magic akin to table turning or pulling a rabbit out of a hat. There's a reason why George Soros called his book on money "The Alchemy of Finance". Just like turning lead into gold or water into wine, in our society the operation of the financial system and the day to day realities of our financial futures have their feet firmly planted in the future of things yet to happen and historically and culturally this is typically the realm of occultism and sorcery. It is exactly this bizarre juxtaposition of the very old world of spirit and culture clashed with such a new flavour of technology creating worlds within worlds to explore that drew me to it in the first place. Divination or the art of divining the future is a very real reality when you work at Goldman Sachs let's just say for the record. If you can't at the very least do a couple of neat card tricks chances are they won't be hiring you on as a trader since peering around dead man's curve is such a big part of the job description.

We live in an extraordinarily industrialised society. The number system is really the true universal language of our culture. Without a firm understanding of the impact that number systems have on our daily lives we lose out to others with a firmer grasp of the fundamentals. When we take control of our own money system we control our own destiny because money literally changes our future when we control it for our own ends. Telephone number Social Security number, date of birth, postcode, it all comes down to numbers. Dollars to donuts. Cradle to the grave.

Learning to trade is like learning to ride a bicycle or tie your own shoelaces. Once you get the hang of it you never need to relearn how to do it. If you doubt the truth of this statement I invite you to participate in a little demonstration of exactly how trading technology really works. Because it's hands-free and completely automated you can use it to generate an additional income stream that will continue to earn you money for decades to come. In an age where it's become essential to adapt to changing times or perish it is a must for professional and novices alike to learn the tricks of the trade, lest they find the way forward in their life coloured by misfortune and penury.

The Way of the Worm

Although algebra can conjure up complex terms and expressions with its hexi-decimals and trinomials what we require specifically is an algorithm which is a type of linear equation that can be explained mathematically as follows :

**If current bar high CLOSE > (greater than) previous bar High CLOSE then buy
If current bar low CLOSE < (less than) previous bar low CLOSE then sell
User definable input = number of trades per direction = equals one. ***

* This third line prevents the system permitting extra positions when a trend runs over several bars in the same direction.

Hey presto. 100% crypotlock or what they refer to in trading circles as being delta-neutral. This is literally in a nutshell the pricing mechanism which secretly runs all the world's financial markets. It is so simple and concise that at first you could be forgiven for thinking that it couldn't possibly be that easy. But trust me when I say that this is as pure as the science behind mechanical trend trading gets. If your dubious as to the veracity of this statement the best step for you would be to go to www.dailyfx.com or google free forex charts (there's lots of them available) , select charting, open up Euro/US dollar, change the time frame to daily and the bar types from candlesticks to simple open high low close, which I prefer. This formula is the cornerstone of modern quantative trading and is known as the algorithmic trading model.

Like knowing Rumplestiltskin's secret name the power vested in price is in my opinion the equivalent of what fire was to a caveman but in a modern world context. Indeed Prometheus stealing the gift of fire from the gods and giving it to the people could not be a more vital analogy to my publishing this book. When you see the world perfectly clearly, and understand just how interrelated and intertwined with the everyday and the banal the monetary system is an epiphany occurs and the true nature of the universe and the big game that is our consensual day to day reality all start to gel together into a model that is cohesive and makes good sense. The modern human as a rational economic being takes centre stage as we realise our place in the universe is innately tied to our ability to control our own economic futures. As Carl Sagan is fond of saying, for me it is better to see the universe as it really is than to persist in delusion, however satisfying that may seem to be".

Although the world financial matrix may itself be very complex with a vast and complex set of factors determining its output, the actual algorithm which controls these many varied economic is the very definition of simplicity itself. In fact it requires only 3 lines to define in logical terms as you can see. Getting this formula into a pc in the form of an automated trading system and hooking it up to a live feed of say the CME euro futures or a spot currency feed is therefore a potentially very clever move indeed.

One of the things that appealed to me about trading in the first place was the fact that it allows you to escape from the confines of a normal working environment and instead telecommute to your co-location server or laptop. This has interesting implications. For example no longer needing to locate yourself where you work but instead being able to live and work anywhere on earth. This gives you maximum flexibility in your lifestyle and if you live in the right place can reduce your taxes to zero. This for me is a huge bonus and one of the major reasons I love to travel about a lot rather than remaining in one location my whole life.

The dollmaker you seek the dollmaker

Now it's important at this stage not to spend money unnecessarily as this is the classic time to make a lot of errors and ignorant mistakes which you'll want to do in paper trading mode so that losses are kept to an absolute minimum. So from here on in its assumed that you are working not live but in paper trading mode in order to save on mistakes. Paper trading mode means that everything is identical to live trading but no actual real money changes hands making it a perfect way to learn. Basically one of the great things about this business is that you can get so much of the groundwork done so cheaply. From leasing Ninjatrader to getting a live broker account for euro futures or spot forex the whole actual expenditure may only be a couple of hundred bucks depending on your skill at being choosy. Although a good broker typically requires a few thousand to open it's not always the case that more upfront buys better quality. I am selling the system I use on my website (www.facedollar.co.uk) which works with Ninjatrader for 50 dollars so you can go straight to that if you get stuck trying to do it yourself. This system works on multiple computers and multiple time frames and instruments making it the perfect tool to trade with. Remember when looking for a broker, that you will probably want to find one that works with Ninjatrader if you want to get your trading to the point of being autonomous and hands-free (there is a list of compatible brokers on their website). As I have said previously I believe being automated to be a very important key step to being consistently profitable and something I highly recommend in place of face time with the system one on one so to speak.

Perhaps you know someone who seems to have the Midas touch with money. Somehow every other move they make turns lead into gold and earns them money. It's a fair bet that this is one secret they keep regarding how they read prices in order to decide how to trade. That and never, ever letting anyone talk you off of your position. Ever, for any reason period. My basic rule of three's for trading anything well then, is as follows.

1. Don't overtrade: You need to get a feel for what has happened historically in the product you want to trade as far as losses are concerned in order to ensure

that you leave sufficient capital to stay afloat. The key to the game is capital reserves. Without sufficient working capital to continue operation the business grinds to a halt. Ultimately this is a level you must decide for yourself based on what you believe will be sufficient. Best is to take the worst historic drawdown and add 50 percent. We can't always afford best practices though so let's leave that one up to discretion.

2. Stick to the plan: Go's without saying. You have a plan or a strategy for trading that you believe will work in the long run. It therefore stands to reason that one of the major factors in your success will be the ability to maintain discipline in the heat of battle that is the daily grind of trading. Jumping off the train because you think you know better this time is one of the surest ways to learn this lesson so don't say I didn't tell you so if this happens to you. Think of the market like shooting a set of raging rapids in a small boat. The rapids contain fast down hills that can get you where you need to go faster. However they also represent certain death if you fail to heed the correct protocols as far as navigating them.

The bottom line is this. Before you go live take the time to open an account with a good futures broker and automate your trading first. This costs nothing but time and a little effort and then you get yourself to the point where your trading now takes care of itself with absolutely no input from you except rolling the contract at the end of a 3 month quarter. This is the cornerstone of good trading because it enforces discipline without which you will not succeed. By using best practices first time we can avoid learning the hard way that we are not approaching the problem correctly. This actually reminds me of my own initial efforts where I used stop orders instead of being automated.

Yes it is possible to send a STOP ORDER instead of using automation. At the beginning of each day just before the market opens you send a stop which is your daily reversal. Let's say we are trading FTSE futures. It may be that I would send the following order at 7:58:00 AM assuming I am short one contract coming into the morning from the night before.

BUY STOP 2 Contracts (1 to close the short and another to get net-long one contract as the system is always either long or short) @ 6375.50 assuming the previous day's high was 6375 and a tick size of 0.50 (the smallest incremental price movement).

This stop resides native on the main LIFFE (London International Futures Exchange) server. This is a very good thing as it means your broker merely provides exchange access and can't mess with your order in any way. Meaning that a bad fill will always be the fault of the exchange and not you're broker ripping you off. The stop will trigger a market order at the price when an order is traded live at that price or worse by someone else first. This saves around 300ms latency compared with the market order created by an ATS potentially resulting in a better price on the order due to less slippage. All this sounds very good so why be automated then?

Simply stated automation is cheap and bulletproof and enforces the one thing essential to success in speculation: discipline. When it's done properly it makes something which is absurdly prone to error almost bulletproof. We need only be sure that the system reinitialises if the server go's down or if the internet times out in likewise fashion. These are both areas already fairly well enforced by the Ninja software itself but we must be completely vigilant in keeping on top of the code. Also there are those who think that it makes sense not to telegraph your orders to the world by placing them on the server as stop orders as I have seen enough deliberate stop hunting in my trading to value the anonymity my ATS implied stops give me when compared with hard stops such as these.

It's a matter of personal taste but personally given how cheaply it can be done to get it automated I would never go back to manually placing orders. It's almost assured that someday you will either get the numbers wrong somehow or put a limit or market order instead of a stop order which will trigger instantly and cost you money. This and the fact that I seem to find myself pulled into making trades that are not part of the plan when I get too much face time with the market is enough to convince me to go the automation route first time as a matter of best practices.

3. Always use stops. Moments of market rotation from long to short or vice versa can be very violent with the market moving hundreds of ticks in a few short hours. It's vital that as a trader you understand that you should always know when and where you will switch your position on any given day and that this eventuality be covered by having a stop in place. Or an ATS that will switch you long to short and vice-versa. Setting an alert that notifies your email or phone when price is approaching your pivot point is also good practice. Otherwise prepare to wake up to a very bad headache when you realise you've failed to change sides and are stuck on the wrong side of a losing trade. Always be thinking in terms of what can go wrong and prepare for the worse at all times are words to live by here.

Now with regards to mental attitude I cannot stress enough the seriousness of the situation at hand. If you break discipline in any way shape or form by overriding the systems signals you are going to lose, and that is going to break your heart. Take it from someone who has been there and knows better. That is why I emphasis getting the system to the point where you are strictly hands off. The discipline in trading revolves around being able to monitor your own thoughts with a view to keeping yourself from ever intervening in the process taking place on your computer. Mark my words this will be the single greatest threat to your continued success and is the key to winning in the long run. The usual pattern is that you think something and reach for the keyboard to do something that isn't hands free, automated trading. This is the critical point where you must remind yourself that you don't know better and cease and desist immediately or else learn the hard way. As I like to tell myself whenever I experience a moment of potential weakness. I don't need to put my hand in the fire to know that it burns.

Some of these software packages are very resource demanding and it's a good idea not to skimp on a computer when you're going to be using it to trade with. Because electricity costs money I recommend using a laptop as it typically draws a lot less power than a desktop computer and this will add up to real savings when you going to be connected to the market for years at a time. As a minimum I would suggest Windows 7 or 8, quad core CPU 3 GHz or higher, 4 GB of RAM. Broadband is essential and very cheap these days. A virtual private server is also good value these days as it takes the system off your hands and puts it in a secure location where no one can get near it making it anonymous and secure. Think of it as a way of removing the business from your home and placing it in a secure containment centre , ghostbusters style, where it won't get in the way of your life. I originally planned to include the ATS system itself with this book but instead I merely describe how to do it yourself. Putting the strategy into action using ninja trader should cost around $100 for a few hours programming for a qualified ninja trader programmer to do for you plus you'll need to purchase the Ninjatrader software as well. I have a website setup at www.facedollar.co.uk where you can purchase the swing trading program from me for 50 bucks to get you started if you require.

Okay so now we are ready to put everything we have learned into practice. We've run the strategy in the paper trader for at least a couple of months in order to ensure that the system is bug free and to get used to the processes involved in daily trading. We've done contingency planning to test what happens when we lose power or our broadband goes down. So now it's time to commit real funds and get the system going for real. It is not uncommon to have brokers literally steal funds from your account if you're not vigilant in keeping a close eye on them so make sure you pick one that is large and stable. You experiment with other brokers at your peril. Best to stick to a large broker such as T.S. or I.B. You have been warned!

In terms of software I have outlined what I consider to be a best of breed combination of Internet-based broker and ATS software in the form of a publicly traded broker and Ninjatrader. Basically the choice of broker is largely up to you since there are a myriad of companies competing within this arena. I especially like brokers that are publicly traded companies such as TS and IB as they offer the protection that comes with size and market dominance. Ninjatrader itself has recently begun offering brokerage services in addition to its platform for using the ATS and is a good compromise choice without the clout of the largest brokers but offering a very competitive service for a cheaper price than even IB is able to compete with. Making it the most price competitive offering of the bunch. If you have to open an account with someone who is anything less than this big I advise you to change to an account with one of these big guys as soon as you can afford it. Really first class execution software, a wide range of products to trade, cheap rates and an excellent API (automated programming interface).

As automated traders it is our goal to create a program which will interact with the automated programming interface to generate automated buy and sell signals which the broker will then execute instantaneously for us. This is our holy grail. I believe I.B. requires 10 K to open an account. However you can immediately withdraw 7/2 thousand this so really you only need to keep around 2 1/2 thousand to begin trading and paper trading and testing the system. Paper trading is an absolute must as it allows you to iron out bugs and get to grips with the realities of being in the market day in day out.

So we decide to setup our test rig to trade a few instruments for us. I will say once again that it is possible to construct a very nice futures trading system using IB's software connected to Ninjatrader and just focusing on half a dozen instruments but for sure you will mostly only require one of these six for your own trading unless you happen to be very well endowed financially. In which case I wish you congratulations and state that you probably don't even need to learn to trade. Dax, Ftse, ES, CL, Euro (CME futures),GBP (CME futures) will do perfectly for our needs. (The original portfolio also contained Sugar, Wheat, Corn, Soybeans, QM mini-crude, 7E mini-euro, Nasdaq, YM Dow Russell futures, Dollar index and GC Comex gold futures.) . This is basically all of the instruments that I'm comfortable swinging overnight at this moment in time. There may be others but these first six of these are my favourites with the euro number one for displaying highest annual returns in terms of ticks and my personal vehicle of choice for the learning trader to get to grips with. Since it is so liquid it's very likely that you could focus solely on the euro and never get any further along than that and that's just fine as well. This list simply represents what's working these days in my profession.

As far as the how to's of getting automated you really simply import the strategy into Ninjatrader. There are some customisable inputs to configure but the whole thing is really simple once you get the hang of it. There's a lot of documentation attached to Ninjatrader that makes my job much simpler by explaining how everything works in detail as well as forums setup to enable system developers to talk shop and exchange ideas. If you purchase the system from my website I am always happy to help you with setting everything up professionally and properly, so it's really no excuse to say that everything is too complex to get to grips with. Attach the strategy to the chart of the daily instrument that you want to trade with the correct parameters configured in the ATS GUI (graphical user interface) and away you go.

It's really best to stick to the beaten track with the choice of instruments that you trade. Subtlety is not a very strong element of the world financial markets. Basic meat and potatoes, keep it simple stupid ideas and execution is the cornerstone of success in this market and wandering off the beaten path to exotic products a definite no go zone. There is simply too much action to be had in these majors for anyone to realistically need to go elsewhere. Also the 24 hour nature of the forex market and some futures such as the E-mini S and P's (the ES) is very preferable to investors as a major geopolitical event could occur at any time. For this reason I tend to push the Euro as a great investment vehicle as well as the ES contract as they both trade round the clock with only an hour gap every 24 hours for the ES contract.

The problem with other indexes and markets is that they can and do gap overnight which is potentially a big problem for us so these are the best 2 markets that I recommend as being most suitable for getting to grips with. The ES is in particular a favoured vehicle since it's so liquid and is a composite of 500 stocks meaning it should be very difficult to manipulate prices of the underlying futures contract. Do yourself a favour and check out timingcharts.com. You will weep when you realise how much action has gone by like the proverbial water under the bridge since oh say 1997 for example in the S and p contract. Oh if I could turn back time.

The best advice is to surround yourself with this information by opening up all 6 charts on your trading platform and make up your own mind which instrument is best suited to be traded by you. If you stick to one of these half a dozen it should be fairly irrelevant as you'll be in good company and surrounded by highly liquid markets that work well and trend strongly. Generally indexes are more consistent than currencies although currencies tend to exhibit higher beta over the course of a year.

The first thing we need to do is use our data stream to build OH LC bars. OHLC stands for open high low close. It is worth noting that since in practice there is no agreed upon universal standard as to how to demark the beginning of a new bar i.e. new day it is possible that some data sources may end up with slightly different results due to the marking of a new day at a different time. Remember to double check that your days are being drawn properly with all of the data and not just some of the daily data as some brokers do (ETH vs RTH data)by cross checking your daily bars with www.timingcharts.com to check that the daily data is the same. Remember to match the correct contract month and year though. Having built our bars we then only need understand how they will move over time. In the case of Ninjatrader, we use one minute bars with a value of 1440 just below the minute selector which creates one day bars for us that are the same as timing charts uses.

Forex : The 21st Century Supermarket

For the sake of simplicity we will deal with the major market currency the Euro-US dollar cross. This is by far the largest market in the world with daily volumes of close to 5 trillion or more than most countries annual GDP. It is also one of the more profitable for exhibiting the highest point gains per year on a daily timeframe. Extensive back testing has led me to conclude that intraday trading by and large does not work and loses money over the long haul leaving us with the daily, weekly and monthly time frames. My testing has concluded that daily has the best beta and so this is what we trade with. This is as a result of seven years of back testing. I call the resulting cyphered number string of profits and losses the crack spread. We can crunch this data into many meaningful numbers. Number of trades. Number of winning trades, number of losing trades, win loss ratio, Sharpe ratio, average win, average loss, average win per trade. This is largely unnecessary for the purposes of this book however.

I've chosen this combination of instrument and timeframe as I feel it represents the best possible exposure to the market for the majority of people and particularly for those who are new to the finance game. The major disadvantage to trading spot forex instead of the futures is that you must pay a small interest charge each day that while not high is irksome and something that futures traders do not have to pay. As a result I prefer futures as they are traded in one central location, not a sprawling assortment of banks as spot is. A lot of testing was required to narrow it down to this.

Along with the ES in the futures market if forms the staple diet of most hedge funds. By simply following the numbers it is possible to deduce this. Two point five million contracts per day traded on average each day as well as almost 5 trillion daily turnover on the Euro means that the market is speaking and is firmly voting with its feet. As I mentioned subtlety does not feature strongly in the trading world. If you find yourself resisting easy answers to your questions like what to trade you may find that it is you who are not thinking about the issue clearly. In this world if it quacks like a duck it's a duck. Far and away the mainstay of hedge fund statistical arbitrage and a great way to get you into the swing of things cheaply.

One useful technique I learned with the ES was to let it get a little beaten up first before launching a contract. It has a point value of 50 dollars and a tick value (minimum incremental movement) of $12.50 so it's possible to get a contract to roll with as little as $2500USD of risk capital although it's probably only around a 50 percent success rate. By waiting until the system has drawn down by say 20 full points (80 ticks) first then we can improve this percentage and in so doing use the systems weakness as our own strength. Taking on the market one contract at a time and then using a fresh account to begin again with another. This is analogous to playing blackjack and counting cards. When the pack gets soft and turns in our favour by drawing down only then do we bet to take advantage of its weakness to improve our chances of success.

The interbank currency market differs from futures in that it doesn't have a centralised market like the eurex or CME exchanges. It is a good all-round performer and a perennial favourite of market traders worldwide. Instead it comprises an affiliation of banks acting as market makers such as UBS, Deutsche bank, all providing liquidity via what is known as the interbank. Personally I like to use futures to trade currencies since the futures market is so heavy regulated and offers all the benefits of spot currency to boot. For this reason we will concentrate on the futures instead of spot currency though both have their pros and cons to contend with.

To better understand the economics involved in trading let's take a look at Ftse 100 futures. £3000 margin maintanence is the minimum account balance required to hold one contract overnight. A 6300 index value times 10 pounds a point (2 ticks @ 5 a tick) equals 63,000 pounds notional value. Approximately 20 percent return on that 63k or around 1250 points annually or 12,500 pounds for an investment of the maintanence plus say 10,000 pounds in risk capital reserves. This means an annual return rate of around 100 percent on your money. Not too shabby, if I do say so myself. These are exactly the kind of economics driving this industry forward in leaps and bounds.

I've got a few ideas about why fear is never far away from the mind of your average big swinging dick on Wall street but its sufficient to say that when trading is a beatable system that anyone worth his salt can outsmart and beat it takes a lot of heart to rise above the rest. I mean it reverses the usual natural order of when a pudgy anorak with a little ingenuity can make more money simply by sitting at home in his size 1,000,000 underpants watching his system do the work for him than 10 of his working-class counter parts can digging ditches .

Trading is not difficult when broken down into numbers. Take a timeframe in this case a daily one. Back tested for a statistically significant period of time say five years. Gives you around 500 trades or approximately a hundred trades per year. Then it becomes like playing a game of blackjack in a casino. Each trade consists of a buy and a sell cycle or vice versa. Think of these 500 trades as being like hands and a blackjack table. Over time we can analyse them and generate information from them which tells us what each hand is worth over time measured as pips or ticks of profit. Then we simply automate the process of playing each hand automatically by programming our trading software to take each trade autonomously and let it run out to infinity. Once we are in profit and playing with house money it becomes a free ride gravy train eeking out a marginal benefit on each trade over time. In my opinion this is the only way to trade and anybody who tells you differently just isn't looking at it and right. As previously mentioned trading is about process control therefore the art of good trading is about programming a computer and then leaving it to do it's job for the rest of your life. Discretionary traders simply waste too much time on a process that has been designed to run automatically using a computer and aren't consistent enough to outperform the market's own internal logic mechanism (ie the invisible hand) over time. In fact if at any time you find yourself exercising discretion in your own trading there is a better than good chance that the system is about to take a lot of your money from you. Never override the system signals for any reason and you will always make money in the long run. It is this one basic truth that causes so much trouble in people's lives.

Which brings us to the black box trading system which I will help you create in this book. It uses a regular computer running Windows to create a state-of-the-art algorithmic trading system that will manage your money for you for the rest of your life completely autonomously. It is precisely the same system used in many most of the world's hedge funds and banks and I will teach you how to build it yourself for less than $100 although that will only allow for trading that isn't live. For live trading you will need to lease or purchase Ninjatrader and that will run you another thousand bucks or so. It is in my opinion the single most valuable skill a person can acquire above and beyond their regular career training most people have to acquire in order to support themselves and their families. So keep that in mind if the prices seem a little on the high side. Try to imagine what a skill like this mightbe worth when contrasted with say the cost of a degree from a college or university. These daily trend patterns repeat endlessly over and over again and are the source of a traders profits.

One of the original titles for my book that I bandied about was Secret Loopholes of the Rich. It is commonly acknowledged that one of the major differences between the rich and the poor is the way that the rich harness the power of the wheel to accumulate capital. As the saying go's speculate to accumulate. It's pretty obvious that the ability to generate a second income to compete alongside ones primary source of income is a huge advantage to have over others. Harnessed properly it is possible to build a second income on the side that will ultimately replace your original occupation and free you from the need to work at all. This was a powerful motivating factor for me let me say that much for sure. I seriously don't need millions of dollars to be happy in my life so much as I need the ability to sustain existence without so much effort on my part to keep everything moving in the right direction.

I had an epiphany at this point as I realised that with just a couple of contracts (like Ftse 100) I could live somewhere cheaply and potentially generate enough income from just basic swing trading to not have to work at all. The epiphany was this. A lot of people dream of becoming rich and assume that they will need millions of dollars in order to have achieved this. This typically leads to a state of despondency as they realise that it's unlikely they will ever possess that much money at any one time. My realisation is that actually what they need is a second autonomous income which matches or exceeds the salary of a normal working person. Then extrapolating that figure over 20 years one can conclude that the key to happiness is not having millions but rather being able to maintain a high standard of living while no longer having to work as hard or in some cases having to work at all. So in other words what is needed is a replacement income rather than a huge amount of money. Then you will be able to enjoy life without the need to work as hard. Of course the harder you work the luckier you get but that's a matter of individual taste.

With specific regards to the barcoding system and its relevance to the subject matter and problem at hand let me say this first and foremost. I need to be quite careful when I draw conclusions regarding biblical terms and passages. Obviously religion is a sensitive subject for many people and everybody has their own way of seeing things. In some ways it reminds me of the hysteria over 3d printing with a lot of the concerns centred on the ability of those with suitable knowledge to assemble a home made weapon like a six-shooter/revolver in their own homes where regulation struggles to reach.

In biblical terms there is reference in the Bible to the mark of the beast. "And that no man might buy or sell, says he that had the mark, or the name of the beast, or the number of his name. Here is wisdom let him that hath understanding count the number of the beast: four it is the number of a man and his number is 600 and sixty six". Gives a whole new meaning to the words predatory pricing but what does it mean exactly? My supposition is that it seems to suggest the potential existence of a cypher or alchemical holy grail that will somehow pave the way forward in one's life with the profits of recurrent speculation if only one had the means and the wisdom to understand its meaning and method of arrangement.

Having devoted a few years to the development of trading systems I now feel certain that it is in fact a reference to one and the same kind of cypher as Adams Smith's invisible hand. You can see that in the same way that Adam Smith realised the one truly valuable item in the whole world was the free floating pricing mechanism that he called the invisible hand which allows for systemic buying and selling over time. All that was required to be wealthy in a capitalist system was therefore this understanding making it a kind of coveted item and an object of extreme desire. Since this is the same number found on the barcode with its 3 jutting sections each corresponding to sixes they are both presumably related to the same knowledge of how to put this specific technique to work.

In other words if you take say the last 5 years of charts for these 6 instruments and applied the code to them it would become clear which made the most money over the period and which was the most reliable. That would then determine how to invest your money the over the next 5 years. If you really want to match wits with what's making money these days since there's a good chance that where the rich put they're money the last 5 years and where they continue to invest over the coming 5 years will be one and the same. The vested interests in these markets are gigantic to say the least and the entire hedge fund industry relies on these numbers for it's bread and butter.

Meaning that you are in very safe company indeed. Once again I repeat that the industry is not at all subtle and the numbers scream where there's smoke there's fire.

Essentially then these arcane references from the bible refer to the secret industrial process at the heart of all pricing in the modern world that carries with it the seed needed to generate wealth over time. In other words a very important part of becoming wealthy, yet vague and shrouded in mystery and innuendo. One of the hallmarks of our society is that we have created an atmosphere of suspicion and vagueness surrounding how the world's financial system works. The process of becoming wealthy therefore starts with a thorough look at how this mechanism works and how we as traders can exploit its inefficiencies for our benefit. For make no mistake it is only through inefficiency that we can hope to turn a profit. It's of no use to us if the end result of our speculations are zero sum. Having defined the parameters then it's now simply a matter of testing different combinations until we find a long number strand that we like enough to trade live.

One comment I come across is what about fundamentals? Many novices ask this question because they naïvely think that big geopolitical events would cause the system to lose money. In actuality the opposite is very often true. In 2008 the world markets fell massively worldwide and the effects of this collapse is still evident today in 2015 due to the sub-prime meltdown and the banking crisis. Yet 2008, the year of the collapse was in fact the most profitable year for the Euro daily trading system system over the testing period. Yeilding over 3000 pips in 2008 alone.

My Kingdom for a computer that plays perfect dominos

It's perhaps not surprising that modern-day trading owes more than a little of its livelihood to modern-day computer hacking and espionage. Looked at objectively there are many parallels between these two worlds that can be drawn. Reduced to its simplest form modern trading involves the penetration of a sophisticated network infrastructure like for example the Chicago mercantile exchange with just one primary offensive tool in your arsenal. In programming terms what is called a subroutine or programming loop. From which the legal term loophole also relates. This Trojan horse program, often called a worm, owes its success or failure to its ability to sustain itself over time. To this end it uses a loophole or subroutine (the 3 line equation) which performs a repetitive action again and again in order to gain a profit from the transactions that it generates over time.

Viewed in this way it's easy to see how much in common an electronic trader, particularly an automated one, has in common with a computer hacker or a spy. For what it's worth it's the modern day equivalent of sending a goldeneye type spy satellite into orbit, albeit in a slightly more modest format. For this reason alone the whole world of trading is traditionally shrouded in a veil of secrecy more akin to the world of espionage than accountancy, and it is not uncommon as a learning trader to have to pick your way through a lot of misinformation and downright lies in order to fulfil your potential. Still with a skeleton key as an icebreaker there is every right to be optimistic at finding a market that will suit you.

This is the key to the law of the conservation of energy as it pertains to your life. The designing of a true perpetual motion machine in order to make physical labour as a means of sustaining economic existence a relic of the past. In so doing freeing yourself from the need to work a physical job and therefore harness a better work play balance by leaving most of the work in your life up to the computer.

Personally I am appalled at how difficult it is to find good information in the world on this subject. Let's be honest here. It simply does not exist anywhere else on the planet but in this book. Don't believe me? Well prove me wrong by finding it then. You will find no reference to the equation I mention in this book anywhere on the planet because the truth is that censorship of the internet is very real in this day and age and we are all victims of it. We are in fact looking at the only piece of information that the world does not want us to possess because it enables us to free ourselves from the need to work and in some cases pay taxes to the state. That fact alone scares the powers that be leading to the bizarre state of affairs where it has become a taboo subject that is off-limits to anybody but the most serious individual investor.

This is quite simply a stunning kick in the teeth and probably the single greatest problem I have with the societal structure as it exists today. I can't begin to tell you what kind of unfortunate situations it creates in the lives of individuals who have to deal with reality through such warped glasses. It quite simply creates an atmosphere of fear and suspicion, which is the very antithesis of an open democratic society which we all supposedly exist in. At the risk of overstating the point I once again paraphrase Carl Sagan with regards to the sad state of affairs we find ourselves in with regards to understanding the financial aspects of life. We have arranged things in our society so that next to nobody understands how science and particularly technology actually works. This is a recipe for disaster on an unprecedented, unimaginable scale. When ignorance and power are set so powerfully in opposition to each other we are all in for a very bumpy ride. Let that be said for the record.

The fact that this info is not in the public domain is so crazy that I don't really know how to explain to people why it can't be found anywhere else in the world or online. It is the original elephant in the room that nobody ever mentions. A true conspiracy of the modern world. When I mention on the back of my book about the barcode and the mark of the beast of biblical revelation I'm not being flippant. I really personally believe that they're both basically a reference to one and the same thing. A cypher such as the one I mention in here that secretly controls the world's networks by utilisation of the algorithm I mentioned. All free-floating market prices move in this way regardless of timeframe or instrument so it's really not that far-fetched to imagine them fulfilling such an extremely vital role in the world economic system. It is the mathematical equivalent of Adam Smith's original invisible hand. This is very sexy indeed as it's like a skeleton key that unlocks every single keyhole in the free market. Simply stated it is a de-encryption key which when applied to daily euro US dollar currency data produces a string of profits and losses over time which I have utilised to create my system.

Getting Even : Beating the big game at it's own game. The inner game of trading.

For what it's worth a good trader is like a good chess player. The sole goal of chess and the sole goal of trading are one and the same. Namely to put the King in checkmate. It's interesting that in chess you don't actually take the king off the board but rather you put it in a checkmate position where it can't move in effect putting it in a position where every twist and turn from then on merely puts it deeper and deeper under your control. This is a perfect analogy to trading where we use every resource at our disposal in an attempt to pawn the King. However it's rarely the case that the king will simply fall straight into your hands. There are pawns which stand between you and your objective. As long as we never lose sight of our objective these can potentially be overcome but the king is clever and will use every means at his disposal to STOP YOU capturing him by depriving YOU of your divine right to rule as his master. If this sounds a little harsh you must understand that we are harnessing a control dynamic that requires one party to the transaction to exist in permanent service to the other.

For this reason there is another level to trading which is the inner game of trading or how to keep fear from running your life. Most often this is referred to as the psychology of trading. It really is beyond the scope of this book to touch very deeply on this subject but it's fair to say that self-doubt is a big obstacle to overcome when you are facing an enemy with such long tentacles. So mastery of the self and of your own mind becomes important to your success. What this really comes down to is mastering your own fears and insecurities. That little voice in your head that tells you why you shouldn't do something or maybe why you should can become very persuasive if you let it. So I will only state that there are very few lessons more important than to remember that only by trying will one ever really learn to win. That and never, ever, ever let your goddam mind talk you into breaking discipline. Suffice to say if there ever comes a time when you're reaching for the keyboard to override your own system you're in trouble and about to lose money big time.

In terms of psychology I like to think of the system as having a logical firewall surrounding it. Trading is instantaneous reaction. Nothing more, nothing less. The smarter you are the dumber you are. The more you think about whether or not to take the plunge and do it the less sure of yourself you're liable to become. It's the kind of logic that walks you in circles wearing down your resolve in the process. This kind of chatter can be hard to overcome because it *never ends*. Therefore aspiring traders take heed, talk is cheap. And actions speak louder than words. At the end of the day the system is fair game and the game is chess. Take it or leave it the goal is to capture the King and in the end your job is to checkmate him. Then every move he makes will only move him into your control. Your opponents King has then become your slave. Like an imp in your computer it will turn ceaselessly for you. Like fire the system is a good servant but a bad master. The King will attempt to use his pawns to outflank you so you must remain resolute and committed to placing him in checkmate at all costs. And keep the internal chatter to a minimum.

Drawdowns. What goes up must come down they say. Of course as tape reading algorithmic traders we fully appreciate the importance of this to our long-term profit earning potential. After all we make money in up or down markets so we really don't care about the direction of the market. Except when they go neither up nor down but instead move sideways. When this happens we are experiencing what they refer to in business circles as having our balls ripped off or otherwise referred to as a drawdown. As surely as prices rise and fall so too will our account equity. Long-term we expect our equity will increase, however in the short term we must be able to anticipate and cover ourselves against loss. Consequently we must have funds available in our account above what we need for basic margin maintenance. Like any other business this working capital must never fall to zero or else our account will liquidate and we will be busted out to use the parlance of the industry.

To get an idea of how much working capital is appropriate we need to examine our seven and half years of back testing data in order to get a feel for historical drawdowns. Looking at our data we can determine what our maximum losing streak was over the testing period . This then forms the basis of our money management or basically how we manage our money in order to stay afloat for the long-haul. Now after a year of operation of the business we may choose to remove the working capital from our profit. Then we move the stop to break even and take the free position.

Picture every chart you see from now on as a traffic light with red and green lights on it. At all times we are other long (buy) green or short (sell) red. So what we want is an ATS that is capable of switching network traffic like a light switch between buy long and sell short. In precise concert with the real-time information flow and millie-second latency on our order fills. Hence the whole point of this book. This kind of trading is actually very common in the modern world. Right place at the right time equals success. Similiar to valve timing in the engine of a car. In order for the piston to turn over smoothly timing is crucial and as traders we rely on split second timing in order to keep our system running smoothly and in precise concert with the overall market dynamic. Which ofcourse it does every time.

One tried and tested technique that trader's employ involves identifying the tipping point. This is the point at which account equity moves into positive territory from negative equity for the last time never returning to negative balance again. This can be very difficult to identify in the short term as it is possible for the account to cross into positive territory for several months only to suffer drawdowns that bring the account back below the demarcation point. Still there is real power when you consider that a $12.50 per pip transaction on the 6E futures contract requires only around $4000 of margin to maintain. By putting the position on with 15 K of risk capital you have a total capital commitment of $19,000 total. You can potentially move your stop to break even after only a few months and take your 15 K risk capital off the table leaving only the accumulated profits and take the free position potentially for the rest of your life. Think of the tipping point as being like an avalanche that starts at the top of a mountain as a small quantity of snow but gathers momentum as it moves down the mountainside picking up more snow and more snow until it becomes a force of nature. As the saying go's, from little things big things grow. This is one of the secrets to momentum investing.

Money management case in point

So we decide to setup our test rig to trade the Euro on a daily timeframe. Vincent Price decides he's going to trade the Euro US dollar cross futures (contract symbol 6E,7E for the half-size) using a daily timeframe at twelve dollars and fifty cents per pip. A pip is 1/100th of a cent and is the smallest incremental movement permitted. This means it is the same thing as a tick in the ES futures contracts. The tick size for the ES futures is therefore $12.50 equivalent to ¼ of an ES full point. His margin maintenance is just under $4000. If his account falls below this number it will instantly and automatically liquidate any open positions and he will have to deposit more funds in order to continue trading. At $12.50 dollars per pip he thinks he will clear around 1.5K per month or 18 K per year. Based on past results from his back testing of 6 1/2 years of data. He deposits US$20,000 meaning he has around 16 K of risk capital and can hence absorb approximately 1300 pips of drawdown before his account will be stopped out and require more funding.

In order to see a live currency market trading I recommend visiting www.dailyfx.com . At the top of the screen you will see a tab marked charts. Click on this and then select euro US dollar and change the timeframe to daily rather than one hour as it is set as default. I like to use simple OHLC bars rather than candlesticks as they are easier to read. Experiment with zooming in and out of bars in order to view them all clearly.

With regards to Ninjatrader there are a few technical quirks to get to grips with. As of this writing Ninjatrader 8 has been released in it's beta format. So we are going to need to avoid it at this stage since it's really only in testing phase. So these instructions should be considered for Ninjatrader 7 only.

By cookie cutting the market into segments like this we create a long-term income stream which is the key to generating trading profits over the long term. This kind of statistical modelling of subsets of data in this way is referred to in technical analysis circles as back testing. Having back tested virtually every instrument that exists in many different time frames I have settled on daily euro US dollar as the main instrument for this book. A match that is better than sliced bread in my opinion.

It's pretty obvious that the ability to generate a second income to compete with one's primary source of income is a huge advantage to have over others in a competitive arena such as we exist in today. The basic caveman requires fire and the wheel in order to prosper. This is something I now acknowledge as basic economic truth. The problem as I see it is everybody is looking at the problem from different perspectives. Leading to a situation where a great deal of confusion develops as to what the best way to tackle the problem.

Of course ultimately for me my experience of trading the system allows me to play my trump card in the form of this book. The experience that I have gained over the last decade has real economic value and by writing this book I am able to potentially teach a lot of people what I have learned in a very cost-effective way. I take that job very seriously so it's been very cathartic to unburden myself of the weight of that knowledge in the form of this book.

This is the key to beating the market. Don't worry about having enough money to trade live. Instead concentrate on learning how to trade profitably as a paper trader and then when you're seeing consistent results and your yearning to go live THEN go ahead and put your money on the line for real. Even then it's a good idea to halve your initial size if you can so any mistakes you make will be cheaper.

The key to understanding what success is like is this. It's possible in this life to spend your whole life working hard at a job you hate until you die without ever tasting any success for your efforts. This is the reality of the world we live in today. The analogy is a car that is stuck in mud with it's tyres spinning furiously without ever gaining traction. If only we can find a nice piece of flat rock and wedge it underneath them we can spend the rest of our lives getting richer. By taking the first couple of steps which may only cost a few hundred bucks to setup and perhaps 15 dollars a month for data fees, we set in motion a chain reaction and take the first tentative steps to financial independence.

Regarding brokers I'm a big believer in finding a good one and then sticking with it. The reason for this is multiple. Lots of customer funds and a great platform with a huge variety of third party applications and proprietary add-ons are what you want. Bucket type operations that offer incentives for signing up are what to avoid at all costs. Do your homework and look for brokers that are publicly traded with billions of dollars of customer funds. That way the incentive for them to cheat and play games with your money will be minimised. Once you become accustomed to the interface and connecting ninja trader and your app to it you will have the whole world of trading at your fingertips. There is a real buyer beware aspect to brokers so be warned. A lot of apparently sturdy brokers are in reality paper thin in terms of capitalisation.

The industry is rife with software issues, downtime and outright cheating so a solid broker is absolutely essential to success. To this end I once again suggest I.B as a large publicly traded company offering everything you need or Ninjatrader brokerage as a potential rival for the mantle of best broker.

And though we may lust and lust. The price we pay in retrospect must surely seem a bargain.

www.ingramcontent.com/pod-product-compliance
Lightning Source LLC
Chambersburg PA
CBHW071017180526
45168CB00003B/1454